TOOLS, NOT RULES:

A WRITING GUIDE FOR YOUNG CREATIVES

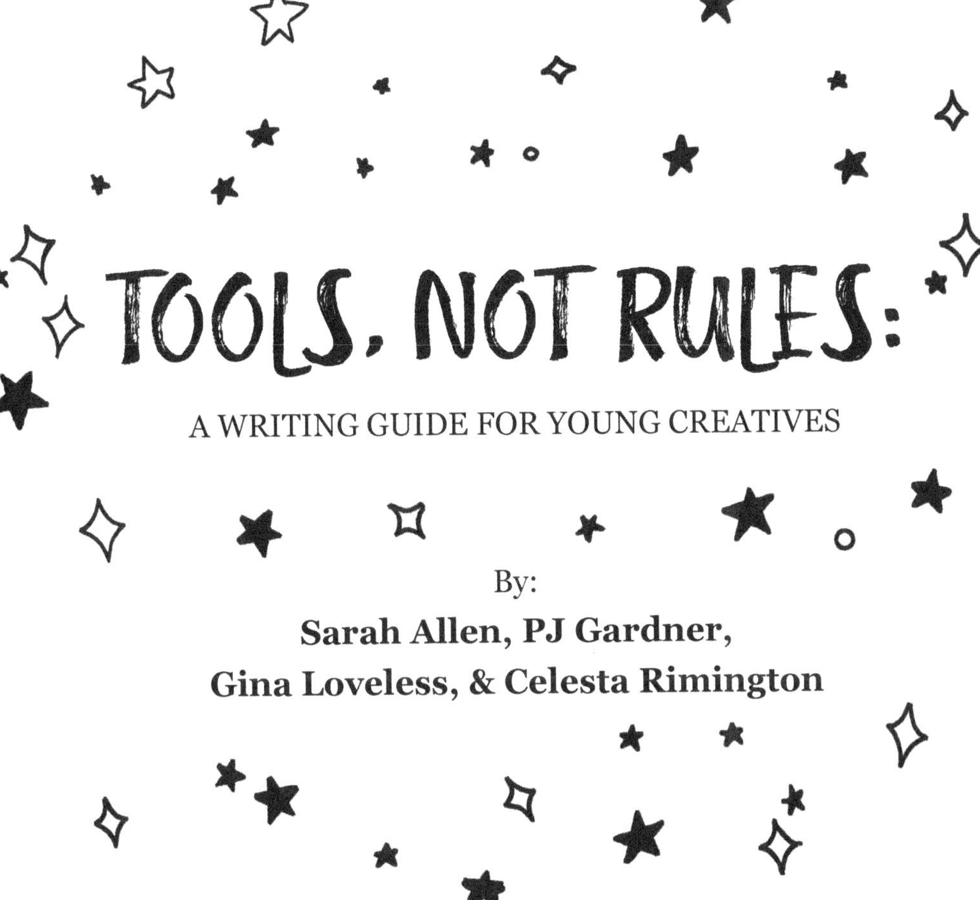

TOOLS, NOT RULES:

A WRITING GUIDE FOR YOUNG CREATIVES

By:

**Sarah Allen, PJ Gardner,
Gina Loveless, & Celesta Rimington**

- To all the students who asked me for this. –Celesta

- For the rule breakers! –Gina

- To all those with storytelling in their hearts. —PJ

- To Grandpa Lambert, for loving words. –Sarah

TABLE OF CONTENTS

A NOTE TO PARENTS AND EDUCATORS

We wrote *Tools, Not Rules: A Writing Guide for Young Creatives* because we care deeply about building a love for writing in children. Like you, we recognize that a creative child is a healthy, resilient child. Unfortunately, today's curriculum offers limited opportunities or resources to teach creative writing, which is why we also wrote this book for you.

A book you can integrate into your lesson plans.

A book you can hand to the eager and gifted writer who desperately wants to jump ahead.

A book to back you up when you tell students that real authors actually have to edit and revise.

A book where the professionals tell all and share the techniques and the art of storytelling like a conversation over school lunch.

To young writers, homeschoolers, parents, guardians, and teachers everywhere, this book is dedicated to you!

INTRODUCTION

Welcome! Welcome dreamers and storytellers, poets and tricksters. Welcome to anyone who has a tale to tell. We've created this book just for you! It's full of tips and advice, as well as activities, that will make writing easier and more fun. And remember that everything we share is simply a tool to help you. Because there are many ways to write a great story.

We can't wait to see what you make!

Now, here's a bit about us.

Meet Celesta

Hi, my creative brains! I'm Celesta. I write magical books about kids having adventures in nature and solving mysteries with their friends. My characters always discover a bit of magic, and they learn something about themselves, too. My first two books are *The Elephant's Girl* and *Tips for Magicians,* and I have many more stories on the way!

Here are some fun facts about me:

- I think research is fun! Finding an amazing fact that I can use in a story is like unearthing a buried treasure.
- My favorite color is blue. It reminds me of the sky, oceans, and lakes.
- My favorite food is Thai food—especially Thai green curry. But I also love Fruity Pebbles!
- I love singing show tunes at the top of my lungs with my son.
- I have a five-pound Yorkshire Terrier named Winston.

Meet Gina

Hey there future writers and movers and shakers! I, Gina Loveless, write humor with heart and help kids feel less alone. My books are *Diary of a 5th Grade Outlaw* (3-book series), *Animal Rescue Friends* (co-author), and *Puberty Is Gross but Also Really Awesome* (nonfiction). My favorite thing about writing is being able to tell stories that mean something to someone else.

A few fun facts about me:

- Favorite color: mustard yellow
- Favorite food: avocado and salmon
- I have a rescue Pitbull named Sasha, and you can find a lot of pictures of my rescue Pitbull Gerdie, who passed away in December of 2022, on my website lovelesswriting.com.

Meet PJ

Hello, lovelies. I'm so glad you're here. I write books about animals, adventures, and mystery. Books like the *Horace & Bunwinkle* series and *The Great Zoodini*. I love writing because it gives me a chance to build worlds and create fun and lovable characters for readers just like you.

A few fun facts about me:

- My favorite color is hunter green.
- I have a Master's degree in Art History.
- Enchiladas are the greatest food ever made.
- I have two Boston Terriers named Rosie and Rocky, and the Universe recently gifted me a kitten called Kaiju.
- I live twenty minutes from Disneyland and twenty minutes from the beach.

Meet Sarah

Hello storytellers! I'm Sarah, and I like writing stories and poems about weird things. Sometimes that means characters who *feel* weird and feel different from other people. Sometimes that means writing stories about scary nightmares coming to life. My books are *What Stars Are Made Of*, *Breathing Underwater*, and *The Nightmare House*. And that's just the beginning of all the fun, quirky stories I want to tell!

A few fun facts about me:

- I have two cats named Morticia and Timicin!
- Like the main character in my first book, I was born with the genetic disorder Turner Syndrome. I know what it's like to feel weird!
- My favorite colors are red and purple.
- I am obsessed with Disney and have done Disney movie marathons lots of times—my favorite is *The Rescuers*.
- PJ is incorrect—German pancakes are the greatest food ever made.

What's the Bright Idea?
Story-Starting Tools
By PJ Gardner

Where do story ideas come from? Do they fall from the sky like raindrops or land on you like butterfly kisses? Actually, ideas can come from anywhere. From your favorite video game or a nature show. From a sign on the side of the road or a song. All you have to do is pay attention, be curious, and ask questions.

Who? What? Where? When? Why? How? And especially what if?

Who invented roller skates?
What is the tallest building in the world?
Where do Komodo dragons live?
When was the battle of Bunker Hill?

Why are there so many ducks in front of that car wash?

How do you make Cheez-It crackers?

What if a duck eating Cheez-It crackers on top of the tallest building in the world and a Komodo dragon in roller skates fought at the Battle of Bunker Hill?

The key is to let your imagination run wild.

And don't worry if your idea sounds like something that already exists. Many storytellers agree that there are only seven types of stories in the world, and we're all retelling them.

Try this. Think of your story like a cheeseburger. It has the basic parts that make it a cheeseburger—meat, cheese, and a bread of some kind. But it's how you put those parts together and what you add that make it unique. For instance, you might put your hamburger patty on a sesame seed bun with cheddar cheese, then add pickles and mustard. While another person might put their patty on a ciabatta roll with gruyere cheese, then add onions, lettuce, and garlic aioli. Both of those are cheeseburgers, but they're totally different. And they're both delicious. And you wouldn't say, "I've had one cheeseburger, so I never want another one." Right? So write your story the way you like it and remember, just like there's room for all kinds of cheeseburgers, there's room for all kinds of stories.

Hmm, for some reason I'm hungry now.

Story-Starting Activities

What if?

Idea SMASH!
By Sarah

Here's a secret about getting ideas...it's ok to get inspiration from the things you like! Maybe you won't exactly write about a girl who finds a place called Narnia in a wardrobe, or a big green angry monster man called The Hulk, but all the things you like to read and watch can give you ideas.

Try this experiment: take two things you really like and SMASH them together. Maybe you really like stories about monsters. And maybe you really like stories about finding secret portals to other worlds. Ask yourself *what if*? What if a girl found a portal to the monster realm? What if a monster found the portal to *our* world? What if a girl realized she was slowly turning into a monster, and what if the only way to stop it was to find the secret entrance to the magic library of healing spells? Now you're on your way to an idea!

Keep a Notebook
By Sarah

In the same way our bodies need exercise, our brains need exercise to help look for ideas! The best way to exercise your idea brain is to carry a notebook. If someone says something funny, write it down! If you have a question about a new billboard across the street, write that down. If you suddenly have an idea about leprechauns taking a bath, write that down too! None of the things you write down have to be smart, clever, or even complete story ideas. Think of it more as a thought-scribbles notebook! But these notes will train your brain to look for ideas and to be curious. Then when you're wondering what to write about, you'll have a whole notebook to look through to spark your imagination!

Diary, But Make it Fake
By Gina

Lots of people write books based on things that actually happened to them, but then they fictionalize parts to make it more humorous or dramatic or horrific. Think about something that happened to you today. Instead of writing down what really happened at the end, ask what would happen if you made something magical happen instead. What if something sad happened to you? Instead of ending it sad, how could you make it funny? Or maybe make it scary?

Research

By Gina

It's probably no surprise that the person who wrote the creative nonfiction section is going to tell you that research is a great way to come up with ideas. But many great stories are actually fictionalized stories of things that really happened. What would happen if you changed the ending to the Moon landing? What if they didn't land on our Moon, but they landed on Venus instead? How would that change things? What would that look like for our space program? Make some fake histories for a new imagined world.

A Picture Is Worth a Thousand Words
By PJ

Sometimes the best way to get ideas is to look at art. Paintings, drawings, and sculptures can offer inspiration we might not have found any other way. Websites like Pinterest, Flickr, and Google Arts & Culture have countless images, so you don't even need to leave your house. But you do need to make sure it's okay with your grown-up to go to those sites.

Now tell a story using this illustration. If no ideas spring up, try describing the image first.

From St. Nicholas (Serial), 1873 by Mary Mapes Dodges

Mix 'N Match

By PJ

Looking for story ideas? Try the Mix 'N Match method.

On a sheet of paper, make four columns: Person/Animal, Place, Genre, and Problem/Obstacle. Then write down six or more things in each column and be sure to number them. (See the chart below for ideas.)

Next roll a pair of dice (or a single die, depending on how many ideas you listed) for each column and write down what you rolled. You might get something like this:

A dragon + Summer camp + Mystery + sunken ship

What story would you tell with those elements?

List of Genres

• Adventure	• Historical Fiction
• Drama	• Horror
• Fable	• Humor
• Fairy Tale	• Mystery
• Fantasy	• Poetry
• Folklore	• Science Fiction

Ask a Friend
By Celesta

Do you have friends who love to read? Maybe you like to talk about books and your favorite stories with some of your friends who read. A great way to jump-start your idea machine is to ask a friend what sort of stories are on their wish list. If they love to read, but aren't writing stories themselves, they will probably have some requests for you. Perhaps they'll ask for a story with dragons and thieves, or maybe they'll say they've been wishing for an animal rescue story that occurs in outer space.

An added benefit to asking a friend is that they know you well, and they might see your writing talent in ways you don't recognize yourself. Your friend may have read something else you wrote and was impressed by your imaginative worlds or loveable characters. Your friends' suggestions might start something in your imagination that you will be excited to write.

Finally, if you ask a friend and build on an idea from their wish list, guess who will be excited to be a beta (or test) reader for you? That's right! You will automatically have an excited reader to give you feedback on your story!

Superpowers List
By Celesta

Grab a piece of paper or your writing idea notebook for this one. Or, if you like, you can use the blank space below for this brainstorm.

What are some superpowers you've heard of in other stories? I've listed a few below to get you started:

1. Animal transformation (able to change into animal forms)
2. Flying (without wings or the aid of any mechanical device)
3.
4.
5.
6.
7.
8.
9.
10.

Now that you have that list, try writing down some superpowers you can imagine but that you haven't seen in any stories. You can take a common superpower and combine it with another one, or you can create something entirely new to you. If you get stuck, one way to do this is to make a superpower very specific. For example, I could have a superpower that allows me to see one hour in the future every Wednesday at noon.

1.

2.

3.

4.

5.

Got your list? Now, think of the most unlikely person to have one of these unique superpowers, and write a story about how they got this specific power or how they discovered it. Think of a reason your character will want to use this superpower. Finally, think of what would happen if your character lost their superpower. How would they feel about that? What would they do next?

Observing Dogs
and Other Character-Building Tools
By Celesta Rimington

Do you have a favorite character from a book or movie? Who is this character and why are they your favorite? Interesting stories have interesting characters! Characters are often human, but you can also write about non-human characters like animals, trees, mythical creatures, or even robots! The important thing is that your character is interesting to you, because then they will be fun to write and read about.

You can find inspiration for fictional characters from real life. Try noticing details in the way people talk, the way they wear their hair, and the clothes they choose to wear. Notice what is important to different people and what they like to do for fun. Pay attention to what people do when they feel different emotions like fear or excitement. It helps to notice these things in yourself, too!

If you want your character to be a real-life person, and you want to write about something they actually did, this is called creative nonfiction. It's important to learn everything you can about this person—including what they looked like, the time period in which they lived, where they lived, and what was important to them. You want to get their story right, so be sure to find detailed and accurate information. You can learn more about researching your real-life character in the chapter on writing creative nonfiction, by my amazing author friend Gina Loveless!

And what if you want to write a story with non-human characters? Oh, this is so incredibly fun! Even with non-human characters, you can find inspiration by observing the world around you. Do you want to write about a dog? Observe dogs and learn about their behavior. Then, try writing what you think a dog would say if they had a voice. What do you suppose dogs think about? Decide what breed of dog your character is, where they live, and their personality. Of course, you also want to give them a great name. Look for more about naming your characters in my character activity on the next page!

No matter which character you choose, here are some important things to discover about your character.

1. What does your character want?
2. Why do they want it?
3. What is your character willing to do to get it?
4. When something gets in their way, what would your character do next?

As you figure out the answers to these questions for your character, your story will begin to form. Your character's voice will show in your writing. They will become an interesting person, thing, or creature that readers will be excited to read about!

Character-Creating Activities

Names, personalities, appearance, motivations...

Name Your Character
By Celesta

Many young writers ask me how I come up with the names for my characters. Here are some of the things I do. Try them out for your characters!

1. Write down names of people you know. What qualities do their names remind you of?

2. Look for baby name books at the library or baby name lists online. Write down names you like. What regions or cultures do the names come from and what do they mean? The background of the names might help you decide what best fits your character.

3. Consider nicknames that might fit your character. What longer name could that nickname come from?

4. Pick a theme that fits your story like nature, the ocean, or a place. Perhaps you want to look for names from Greek mythology or from popular movies. Search online for baby name lists that fit these themes.

5. The Social Security Administration website will let you conduct a search of popular names from specific years, decades, and locations. Try typing in the year you were born and choose a location where you might want to set your story.

https://www.ssa.gov/oact/babynames/

6. Look at maps and find names of cities, rivers, mountain ranges, and lakes in different parts of the world. What do the names mean? Are any of them a good option for your characters?

7. Just make one up!

Won't You Be My Neighbor?
By Celesta

As Sarah mentions in her Four Corners of A Strong Character activity, relationships matter! So much of who your character is will be revealed through their relationships with other characters.

Think about the way your main character interacts with others. Is your character the leader of their group of friends or do they prefer to stay quiet or follow along? Does your character have a friendship with their next-door neighbor, or do they have a neighborhood feud over who makes the best lemonade?

Write a few sentences about your main character from the point of view and in the voice (style of speaking) of:

Their best friend:

A neighbor:

A sibling:

The antagonist (the character who works against your main character's goals):

Once you've done that, write what your main character would say about each of those same people. Be sure to use your main character's point of view and voice (style of speaking) below.

Their best friend:

A neighbor:

A sibling:

The antagonist:

What did this exercise reveal to you about your characters? Did you learn more about who they are and the way they think? You probably discovered something that matters to each of these characters and why they act the way they do.

Character Development
By PJ

I believe a main character should grow and learn over the course of the story, so when I write I always start with these two questions, "Who is the main character at the start of the story and how have they changed by the end?"

For example, in *Horace & Bunwinkle*, Horace the Boston Terrier starts off hating the farm where his human has moved him. By the end he comes to think of it as home.

Now, who is your main character when the story begins? And who are they at the end? What have they learned? How have they grown?

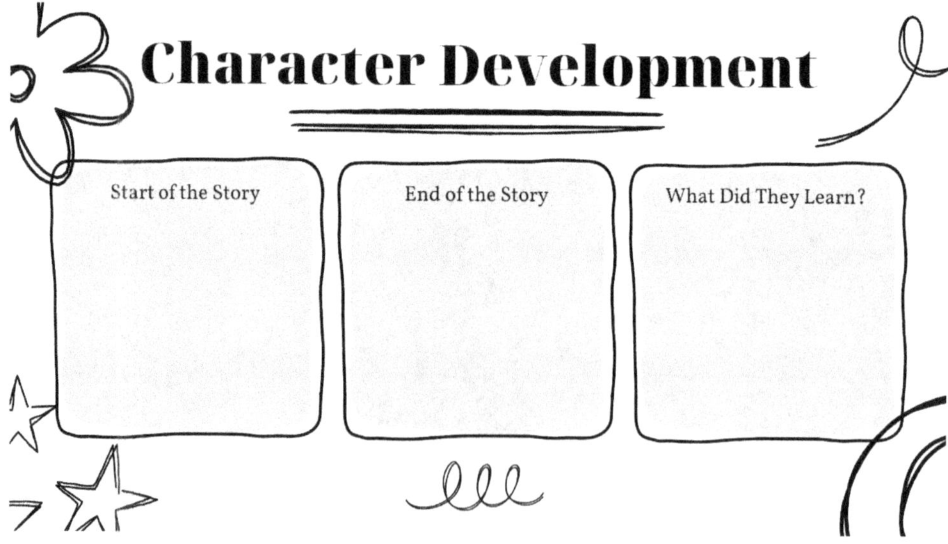

(Hint: you can use this character development to help you plot. After all, your character will have to be in situations that force them to face their fears and dreams.)

What's Your Sign?
By PJ

Looking for a fun way to get to know your character better? Check out their astrological sign, Myers-Briggs personality type, or Enneagram number. Then use what you find to help you develop your character. There are many places online that can help, but always check with your grown-up before looking anything up on the web.

For example, the astrological sign of Gemini is known for being charming and talkative, but also quick to change their minds. The Myers-Briggs Personality type ISTJ is described as responsible, hard-working, and down to earth. Enneagram 6s are said to be loyal, dependable, and good at anticipating problems.

Now pick one and write a character with those traits:

The Four Corners of a Strong Character
By Sarah

There are four basic ingredients to creating a strong character. If you can answer these four questions, you are on your way to writing a character your readers will remember!

Want: What specific thing does your character want more than anything else? Do they want the perfect dress for Prom? To catch the monster under the bed? To slay the dragon? To learn to fly the spaceship? The more specific and concrete the better!

Backstory: Why does your character want that specific thing? Why does it matter to them so much? You don't have to include every bit of this in your story, but it's a helpful thing for you, the author, to know.

Relationships: Who do they care about most? Maybe there's a big group of people they care about. Maybe just one person. But when we know who your character cares about, we understand them more!

Quirks and foibles: What makes your character stand out? Do they have a particular way of speaking? A particular outfit they love to wear? An obsession with velociraptors? Let us know what makes your character unique!

Use YOUR Ingredients!
By Sarah

The stories you write are stories only *you* can tell, and that's the same for characters! Think of it this way: if you and your friend both wrote a story about a pirate queen, they would still be very different characters, even though they're pirate queens! Same thing if you wrote about a baker or a spaceship captain or twin sisters on their first day of school. They'd be unique, and that's because *you're* unique. So, start by asking *yourself* some questions:

- What are my obsessions?

- What makes my family unique?

- What is my biggest fear or worst nightmare?

- What makes me weird (in the best way!)?

- What special stories does my family tell?

- What kind of friend am I? An upbeat cheerleader friend? A quiet good-listening friend?

- What is my most important memory?

These are a few questions you can ask yourself to figure out what makes your writing unique. What would happen if you picked one of these questions and gave your answer to your character?

Describe Your Character
By Gina

Something I like to do when I'm stuck with a character's attributes is to answer a boatload of questions about them. Use these questions to figure out the details of your character. I'll name 10 questions here, then you name 10 more.

1. Name?
2. Race?
3. Eye color?
4. Hair color?
5. Do they wear glasses?
6. Do they have any disabilities?
7. What's their favorite thing to say?
8. Favorite food?
9. Favorite color?
10. Is their family big or small?
11.
12.
13.
14.
15.
16.
17.
18.
19.
20.

Interview Your Character
By Gina

Close your eyes and imagine that you are the host of a late-night TV show or the next big podcast. You're about to interview the main character from your book. What questions would you ask them? How would they answer? Write the back and forth on the page below.

How Did the Ducks End Up in the Police Car?
Tools for Plotting Your Book
By PJ Gardner

So you have an amazingly cool character and an awesome story idea. Now, you need a plot. A plot is what happens either to your character *or* because of your character. It's really just a series of events with a beginning, middle, and end.

There are roughly six elements to a plot, which I'll explain using Rick Riordan's *Percy Jackson & the Lightning Thief.*

- Exposition - the beginning where we are introduced to the character and their world/situation.

  Percy Jackson is a struggling twelve-year-old boy attending a school for troubled kids.

- Inciting Incident - the person or event that forces change into the main character's life.

On a school field trip Percy is attacked by one of his teachers, who is actually a mythological Fury in disguise. Afterward Percy discovers he's actually the son of the Greek god Poseidon and must go to Camp Half-Blood, where he can train with other demi-gods.

- Rising Action - a series of incidents that drive the story forward.

While he's training at Camp Half-Blood Percy is accused of stealing Zeus' lightning bolt. Percy teams up with Grover the satyr and a daughter of Athena named Annabeth to find the bolt and stop a war between the gods. Along the way they cross the country, battling monsters as they go.

- Climax - the moment everything leads up to.

The trio confronts Hades, who they believe is the true thief. But it turns out someone has stolen from the god of the underworld as well. Hades accuses Percy of being the thief.

- Falling Action - the events following the Climax that resolve questions and situations from earlier in the story.

Percy and his friends escape from Hades. Later they discover Ares, the god of war, has the stolen items. He claims to have taken them from the original thief. The heroes manage to take the items back and return them to their owners, thus stopping a war.

- Denouement - the ending where everything is resolved.

  After saving the day Percy learns that another camper, in league with the titan Kronos, was behind the nefarious plot. And they aren't done yet.

Trying to think of all those pieces may feel overwhelming, but don't worry. You don't have to know all of that before you start writing. Now some people do, and they're called Plotters. Other people know a few key details and figure it out as they go along. Those people are called Pantsers (as in they write by the seat of their pants) or Discovery Writers. Both are perfectly acceptable but do know that at some point you will need to organize your story.

We'll explore plot structure more in the activities.

Plotting Activities

Discover what happens in your story

Try, Try, Try
By Sarah

Plot is what happens when your character goes for what they want. How do they do that? What do they try, and what happens? What's stopping them from getting the thing they want?

Write or draw whatever is stopping your character from getting what they want!

Yes, But / No, And
By Sarah

Feeling stuck in your story? "Yes, But / No, And" can help you get unstuck.

Your character wants something, and is trying to go for it, right? Well, did the thing they tried work? **Yes, *but*** now that's created a new problem they have to solve. Or **no, *and*** now the problem has gotten even worse!

For example, let's say our plot is about a monster fighting ninja who wears hearing aids. What she wants is to stop the monster from wrecking the entire school! She tries setting a trap. Does the monster trap work?

- **Yes, *but*** now the monster's much bigger mother has come, and she is angry!
- **No, *and*** our ninja fighter lost her hearing aids, so now she can't even hear which way the monster went next!

Try it with your own story!

Think General
By Gina

Take the plot from one of your favorite books. What happened in that plot? Did a character go to a school and learn a lesson? Did a bad guy wreck the good girl's plans, but then the good girl came back and defeated them? Use that general plot but put your specific character in that story. What changes? What happens to your characters?

Practice Makes Better
By Gina

Learn how to plot better by learning how your favorite books were plotted. While you're reading your next book, write down "Chapter 1" and then in only one to two sentences, write down what happens in that chapter. Then do the same thing for the next, and the next. By then end of the book, you'll be able to see the entire plot for that book. What can you learn from this? What can you use while plotting your book?

The Hero's Journey
By PJ

One of the most common plots around the world is known as the Hero's Journey. Harry Potter, Percy Jackson, Luke Skywalker, and a whole bunch of other characters have lived out this plot structure. In this exercise, I'll use *Disney's Moana* to explain in more detail. (CONTAINS SPOILERS!)

- The Ordinary World - Where it all begins. The main character's everyday life.
  Moana's life on Motunui.

- Call to Adventure - Person or event who brings change or a choice to the character.
  Motunui is dying and the ocean is calling so Moana sets out to save her people.

- Refusal of the Call - No way, says our hero/heroine.
  Moana resists the ocean's pull at first, but then gives in.

- Meeting the Mentor - A wise guide appears.
  This could be two different people here. Moana's grandmother and Maui. One guides Moana on a spiritual/personal journey, the other guides her on a physical journey.

- Crossing the First Threshold - Our character leaves behind their safe, familiar world.
  Moana takes one of the ancestor's boats and sails off to defeat Te Ka.

- Tests, Allies, Enemies - Hero/heroine gathers friends, foes, and failures.
  Moana meets Maui, who is an ally. They face the coconut monsters and the giant crab Tamatoa.

- Approach to the Inmost Cave - Danger rises and the hero faces defeat or a major obstacle.
  Maui and Moana fight Te Ka and lose. Maui is injured and the boat is destroyed. Maui abandons Moana. Grandmother appears and Moana discovers who she is.

- Ordeal - The biggest challenge/struggle of the main character's life where they face their greatest fear.
  Moana returns to fight Te Ka again. Maui returns to help.

- Reward - The lesson learned, power gained, or artifact attained.
  Moana learns that Te Ka is really Te Fiti. She returns the goddess' heart.

- The Road Back - It's not over yet. The Hero has to deal with the fallout of the Ordeal. (This can be good, too.)
  Te Fiti gives Moana a new boat.

- Resurrection/Atonement - The final test/battle for our main character.
  Hmm, I don't think there is one in Moana.

- Return - Our hero/heroine heads home again, changed and victorious.
  Moana returns to her island which is healthy and alive

again. Then, she leads her people back out onto the ocean.

Now it's your turn. Write out a plot using these twelve steps/stages. You can use the lines below or your own notebook.

It's a Mystery!
By PJ

To write a mystery you need six things:

- A detective or investigator - character(s) who sets out to solve the mystery
- The misdeed - the crime, problem, or secret that needs to be solved
- A culprit or culprits - the wrongdoer, the one who did the misdeed
- Suspects - possible culprits
- Clues - hints or evidence of who's behind the misdeed
- Red herrings - false clues or trails that lead the detective in the wrong direction.

.. PJ says:

The term red herring supposedly comes from a hunting practice. People would smoke herring fish, which would turn red, and then drag them over the ground in order to throw hunting dogs off the scent of their prey.

Make a chart like the one below, fill it in, and . . . presto! You've got everything you need to plot your mystery. I recommend having at least two suspects, three clues, and one red herring.

Three Tries!
By Celesta

When your main character confronts the central problem of your story (whether it's a problem with a friendship, a problem in nature like escaping a wild animal, or a problem with an enemy), it can make the story more fun to read if they don't succeed the first time. If you're writing a story where the problem gets resolved at the end, try giving your main character three tries before they succeed.

As you structure where things happen in your story, it can make your plot stronger to have your main character go through the hardest, most discouraging part of their journey after trying at least two times to solve the problem. Then, in that hardest moment (often called "the dark night of the soul") they'll realize why their first two attempts to solve the problem didn't work. They will learn something that they didn't understand before. They'll grow and change. And that's when your main character might discover the third solution that finally works!

If you want to use this "three tries" tool, use the list below to guide you. Then, make your own list and fill in the details of your main character's two tries and failures, what their ultimate challenge will be, what they realize or learn, and their final try that wins!

Three Tries:

Try number one = fail
Try number two = fail
Big ordeal or darkest despair
Realization and plan (perhaps gather allies)
Try number three = win

Why Them?
By Celesta

This exercise is just as much about character as it is about plot, but it will help you with both!

Write your plot in one or two sentences, as if you were explaining it accurately, but briefly, to a friend. For example, I would describe my book *Tips for Magicians* by saying:

A boy who recently lost his mom moves to a desert art village to live with his aunt. He learns that the winners of the annual art contest win a magical wish, but the wish-granting muse has gone missing.

Try this with your story. Then, ask yourself this:

Why is my main character the right one for this particular story? Why are they the one to go through this experience?

In *Tips for Magicians*, the boy in the story is dealing with grief from losing his mom in an accident. He wishes his dad wouldn't be so sad so they could be more of a family. Why is this boy the right character to look for the missing muse that used to grant wishes? Because the muse in the story is sad, too, and needs someone who will understand that and find it. My main character can relate to the problem and is best able to help. The thing my main character wants (a wish) is going to require him to face something that is hard for him.

So, why them? Why is your main character the one that belongs in your plot? They need to be the one who'll eventually provide a good solution to the problem, but they also need to have lots of ups and downs to get them there.

Make a list of your main character's strengths and weaknesses. Include their fears, too. **Then, make a list of things that happen in your plot (or could happen)** that will be the biggest challenge for someone like your main character. For example, a shy girl who gets stage fright also loves animals. She might have the best ideas to rescue a bear that is being held captive by some cruel people. But, in order to get the help that she needs to rescue the bear, she has to give a speech in front of a lot of people. She'll have to face her stage fright to solve the problem.

As you plot your story, give your main character a chance to face their weaknesses and do hard things. Your plot will be stronger, and your character will grow to become the best one to solve the central problem and be the hero at the end!

Lost in Space or Lost at Disneyland?
Setting and Worldbuilding Tools
By Celesta Rimington

If you're a writer like me, you might get your ideas from imagining unique places and different worlds. Maybe you get ideas because you visited someplace new that inspired your amazing, creative brain! But even if you get your ideas from thinking of characters or a plot first, you'll eventually need to create the setting for your story. This is where your characters live. The setting is when and where your plot happens.

Let's start with the type of story you're writing. Does your story occur in our real world or a fantasy world? Does it take place today, in the past, or in the future? A good way to start is to decide what place and time will give the best environment for the kind of story you want to write.

For example, let's say you're writing a story about friends having an adventure, and they get lost. Decide if you want the friends to be lost on a mountain trail, at an amusement park, on an intergalactic journey, or in a magical forest. Do they get lost in the summer or the winter? Is it daytime or nighttime? What is the weather like? Your answers to these questions will begin to create your setting.

Now, think about how your story would change if your lost friends live in the past, present, or future. This will determine whether or not they can use a cell phone or the internet or if they travel by horse-drawn carriage, cars, or spacecraft. The time period of your story will also affect the way the characters speak and maybe even the money they use.

I am a BIG fan of setting, and I love deciding all these details and building worlds. But if any of this feels tricky to you, I have a suggestion. Think of a place you've been that you know really well—perhaps your school or a grandparent's house. Describe that setting and choose a season, a time of day, and the weather. Now, write a scene with your characters in that setting.

If writing a setting is easy for you and you want a challenge, I have a fun exercise for you in the activities to help you create new worlds—perhaps even magical ones!

The awesome thing about setting and worldbuilding is that you are the creator! You get to decide not only what happens to your characters but when and where it happens. Your imagination can take you and your characters anywhere!

Setting and Worldbuilding Activities

Writers get to create worlds! Have fun with it!

Draw a Map
By Celesta

It helps with your setting if you know where things are located in your story. Draw a map of your setting. You don't have to be an amazing artist to do this! All you need is a paper and pencil.

Here's a picture of the zoo map that I drew in my notebook when I began writing *The Elephant's Girl*. If you've read the book, you'll see that the zoo underwent some changes as I worked on the story, but this is how I started.

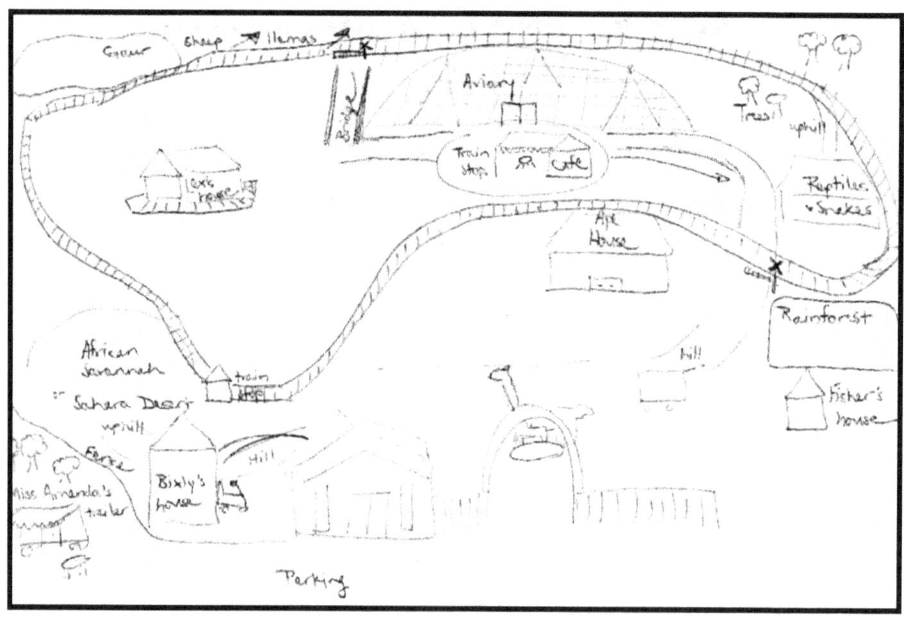

Sketched map of the Lexington Zoo as drawn in Celesta's writing notebook for her novel *The Elephant's Girl*

In your drawing, show where all the important scenes take

place. Your map could be the layout of the inside of a house, or it could be the streets and buildings of a town. It could also be as big and detailed as the geography of a fantasy world.

If you are creating a fantasy world, try including things like rivers, towns, wilderness, and travel routes. Are there deserts or forests? What is the weather like? Are there oceans or seas? Look at a real map to get ideas.

Now, use your map as a guide while you write your story. This will help you have a better picture in your mind of where the characters are and what living in their world is like for them.

Worldbuilding With the Senses
By PJ

Whether your story takes place in the school library, on Mars, or in a world created from your imagination, you can bring it to life through the five senses.

1. What does it LOOK like?

2. How does it SMELL?

3. Are there specific SOUNDS?

4. How do certain things FEEL?

5. What does the food TASTE like?

For example, if your story takes place in the school library:

1. The room is round with bookshelves about halfway up the wall. Above them are posters of famous book covers.

2. Normally, it smells kind of dusty, but today it smells sour—like someone threw up and they used that weird powder to clean it up. (This one does double duty—it tells the reader that something is different today, and that could be important to the story.)

3. It's weirdly quiet, too. Usually, there's a teacher or kid in here talking to the librarian, but I'm the only one here.

4. I head to the shelf where the graphic novels are. Ms. Jax said I could check out one when I finished my book report. Suddenly, the room grows cold. I shiver as a wall of ice forms around me.

5. I gasp and taste frost on my tongue. What's happening?!?

Now you try.

Scene and Setting Mash-up
By Celesta

A great way to sharpen your setting and worldbuilding tools is to experiment! It doesn't have to be perfect because you can always revise later. Try this one out:

1. Choose a scene to write. Decide who the characters are, what they want, and what is getting in their way.

2. Now, write that scene set in your school, during the school day, in October. How does the time of year affect what happens? How does being at school influence what the characters can do and what they notice with their senses? How does the school setting add to the conflict?

3. Now, choose a completely different place and time, and write the same scene with the same characters in that new setting. You could choose your own backyard, the mall, Antarctica, or maybe another planet. Use your imagination and have fun. When you're finished, ask yourself: How did my scene change from the first one? What new things are exciting and what is challenging? What do the characters have to do differently?

4. If you enjoyed that, try just one more setting and make it very different from the first two. Which of your settings do you like best for your scene?

Make the Environment a Character
By Gina

Imagine the setting of your world is a character in your book. As you read through what you've written, imagine what it would say about how the characters are treating it. How might the setting react to what's happening in it? Can you add any of that into your story?

Make the Environment a Character Part 2
By Gina

Okay, so you've thought about your setting's motivations, but have you fully described your city or rural landscape or wherever, like you would your character? Each time a character enters the room, have you integrated a description of the room into the writing? Try writing a paragraph description of every place the character visits, and then see how you can integrate pieces of that into your writing.

Abracadabra – Create a Magic System
By PJ

Fantasy is one of my favorite genres. I love all the details that make the world and the magic feel real. There are some big questions to ask when building a magic system.

- Who uses magic?
    Only a select few?
    Everyone?

- What does the magic do?
    Heal?
    Curse?
    Does it make life better or worse?

- What can it NOT do?
    Kill?
    Bring back the dead?
    Change appearance?

- Is it dangerous?

- Is something special required to perform magic?
    A wand?
    A special ring?

- How does using magic affect them?
    Make them tired?
    Age them?
    Turn them evil?

- Is Magic kept secret or does everyone know about it?

- Are there special ceremonies, languages, or clothing for magic users?

- What does your magic look like?

Now and Then
By Sarah

The way you describe the setting in your story depends a lot on how your character *feels* about that setting. And those feelings might change!

Then	Now
Describe your character's bedroom on a day when she's really angry. Maybe something happened at school that upset her. Maybe she had a fight with her mom. How would she describe the room when she's feeling that way?	Now describe your character's bedroom on a day when she's really happy. Maybe it's her birthday. Maybe she just made a new friend, or got the lead role in the school play. How would she describe her room then?
Describe the weird neighbor's house from the point of view of when your character was very little. She thought the house was tall and spooky, and the neighbor was kind of creepy. How else would she describe the house?	Now your character is older. She's met the weird neighbor lady, who turned out to be...pretty nice! Now how does she feel about the house? How would she describe it?
Describe your character's grandma's house. Maybe your character has been there lots of times before, and everything is familiar. How would she feel about that house?	Now imagine that your character's grandma has sadly passed away. Now how would your character feel about the house? How would she describe it?

Whether your story is set in our world, on a spaceship, or in a fantasy land, the way your character feels about where they are matters!

Earth With a Twist
By Sarah

Do you want to create a unique, magical world, but feel like you don't even know where to start? Don't worry, I feel the same way. One of the best places to start is by taking what we know–planet Earth–and giving it a twist. Pick just *one* thing to change. What if dragons existed in New York City? What if the Yellowstone volcano erupts? How might that change the climate and economies and even governments? What if Japan never bombed Pearl Harbor? What if a new mineral is discovered that gives people the ability to read minds?

The possibilities are endless! Once you pick your twist, think about how that would change other things. You're only making one change, but that change ripples out and influences other things as well. Now you've got a setting like no one else's!

CHAPTER 5

Say WHAAAAAT?
All About Dialogue
By Gina Loveless

Are you a talkative person like me? You might like to talk to everyone you meet, like the mailman, your teacher, you friends, or new kids you meet at the park. You can't wait to tell them about the next big idea you have or even just what the weather is like.

Or maybe you're less talkative. Maybe lots of ideas whirl through your brain, but you don't say them out loud. When people talk to you, you listen deeply, and process what they're saying, but you don't feel the need to say much to them.

These are two different ways to approach dialogue: external dialogue and internal dialogue. External dialogue is all the things people say out loud and internal dialogue is the thoughts people have. Both of them help move the story forward.

Some good questions to ask yourself about external dialogue when writing a story are: Does this sound natural? Would people really say this?

A simple way to check to see if the external dialogue you've written sounds natural is to have a friend or family member read it out loud.

Questions to ask yourself with internal dialogue are: Why are they thinking about this? How do these thoughts help move the story forward?

In a technical sense, external dialogue is when you see this in a story:

"I want scrambled eggs for dinner," said Julie.

When a character is processing thoughts through their head, they might look like this:

Julie thought, *I really want breakfast burritos for dinner, but I don't want to be rude.*

Now check out the exercises on the next pages to test out your dialogue skills.

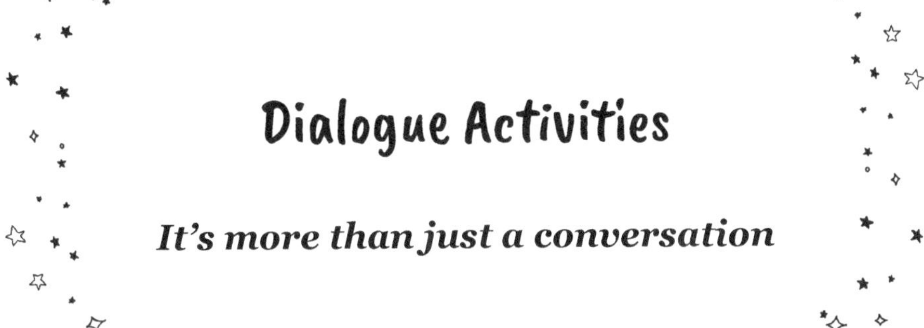

Dialogue Activities

It's more than just a conversation

Practice Dialogue by Interviewing Your Character
By Celesta

Choose a character from your story and write a question for your character to answer. Then, write what you imagine they would say back to you. Write it as though you hear their voice. Write exactly the way they would talk to you, instead of worrying about perfect or complete sentences. Now, write what you might say back to your character. Have a conversation with your character on the page. This is dialogue! And you're learning more about your character at the same time!

For example, a character interview I might have with Lexington Willow from *The Elephant's Girl* could go something like what you see below. (For this activity, I wrote it as dialogue with punctuation and dialogue tags.)

"If you had to pick your favorite vacation, what would it be?" I asked.

"Does it have to be a real one?" Lex asked.

"I guess not. I mean, I was interested in knowing where you've been, and what you liked about it," I said. "But if you want to tell me an imagined vacation, I guess that's okay, too."

"I'll tell you an imagined one," Lex said. "Because I've never been on vacation away from the zoo. But I sometimes imagine where I would explore with Fisher. *If* I got brave enough to go, and *if* Fisher stayed out of trouble long enough."

Listen to Conversations
By Celesta

This activity is fun and useful, but it can also be tricky! It's important to ask people if it's okay with them if you listen to their conversations. You aren't going to use their exact words in your story, but you are learning how to make your dialogue realistic by paying attention to actual conversations.

Try asking some family members or a group of your friends if you can make notes while they talk. You can reassure them that you won't use the actual conversation in your book. This is for research purposes. It will help you to notice how people communicate by what they say and what they don't say. Some communication is done through facial expressions and gestures. Sometimes people say a lot about how they're feeling by not answering at all. Notice how dialogue changes depending on the setting, the ages of the people, and what they are talking about.

Rewrite Dialogue
By Gina

Pick one of your favorite TV shows. Is it your favorite because it makes you laugh out loud, or because it makes you cry? No matter what it does, there was a writer sitting in a room, crafting the lines that the character says. Practice writing the dialogue you hear on your favorite show. Literally copy down, word for word, exactly what they say. Then, read it out loud. What makes it funny? What makes it emotional?

Highlight Dialogue
By Gina

One way to learn to write strong dialogue is to learn from the greats. Pick out one of your favorite books on your shelf. (Don't pick a library or school-owned book for this one.) Then, grab a highlighter from your school supplies or ask your parent or guardian if you can use one from their office/ work/ home supplies. Go through the book, and as you're reading it, highlight every line of dialogue (internal or external) that you come across. Once you're through the book, read the highlighted sections over again, and see what makes them work so well.

Pass the Potatoes
by Sarah

A lot of different things influence the way people talk. For example, where is your character from? Are they modern, or from a different time period? How old are they? Are they rich or poor? All of these things might change the way your character talks, even in small, simple ways. A spoiled six-year-old will speak very differently than a poor 14th century milk maid.

For example, how would each of these characters ask someone to pass them the potatoes?

King:

Pirate:

Modern teenager from a poor Chicago family:

Middle-aged midwestern farmer:

Rich debutant from the 1920s:

You:

Hidden Messages
By Sarah

As you've done the awesome interviews and listening suggested by Celesta and Gina, maybe you've noticed something–people don't always say *exactly* what they're thinking, or *precisely* what they mean. Sometimes they only hint at it, or sometimes they say the opposite!

For example, maybe you've had a day at school recently that wasn't the greatest. Then when you got home, your mom or dad might have asked, "How was school?" Maybe what you said was, "Fine," when what you were really thinking was, *my favorite socks got ripped on the playground, I dropped my sandwich on the disgusting lunchroom floor, and pretty sure I did not get an A on that math test*. This kind of thing happens all the time! Both in real life, and in books. In fact, these hidden thoughts behind the words are probably *more* normal than saying exactly what we're thinking!

Try this out in your story! In the next scene you write, when your characters talk to each other, think about which ones are bolder and blunter. Which ones have a harder time saying exactly what they mean? And what are they thinking? What are the hidden messages behind the words? When your reader can see the differences between what your character says versus what they think, it will make your character seem real, and pull the reader into the story!

How Your Character Talks
Says a Lot About Them
By PJ

Dialogue is a great way to show your character's personality–from the words they use to the way those words are written on the page.

If your character loves dinosaurs, they're probably going to know all kinds of things about them. And they're definitely going to drop that into regular conversations. For instance, everyone is talking about how their teacher, Mrs. Jones can't reach the top of the dry erase board. Your character might say something like: "That's just like the T-Rex. They've got super short arms and only two fingers on each hand." And when they get scared, they could shout, "Holy Cryolophosaurus!" Or, if someone who isn't very smart is mean to them, they could say, "That guy's such a stegosaurus."

Say your character talks really fast because they're one of eight kids and they have to go fast, or they can never get a word in. Their dialogue might look like this:

"Wehavetogetinlineforlunchorwe'llmissit."

Or if they speak slowly because they need to take time to think things through, you could write it like this:

"Well . . . maybe . . . we . . . should . . . do . . . that."

Maybe they're really loud.

"MRS. JONES SAID BE QUIET OR WE'LL ALL GET IN TROUBLE!"

Here's your exercise, think about two of your characters—what they love, how their minds work. Now, write a scene where they're scared.

Internal Dialogue
By PJ

In this activity, we're going to take Sarah's idea about hidden messages a step further by playing with internal dialogue. Not everyone is chatty. But just because someone doesn't say a lot, doesn't mean they aren't thinking a lot. That's where internal dialogue comes in.

I'm going to give you a situation where a character doesn't say what's on their mind.

And you can write out the scene in your notebook.

··· **PJ says:**

Remember that internal thoughts look different on the page than spoken ones.
<u>Spoken</u> - indent, quotation marks, possibly a dialogue tag.
"Very funny, Finn. Now where's my hat?" Lena said.
<u>Unspoken</u> - indent, italicize.
Finn is such a jerk! Why does he keep taking my hat?

1. The character desperately wants to be liked, so they don't share their doubts about a plan to break into the teachers' lounge.

2. A student has moved from another country and doesn't

speak the new language well. They want to make friends, but don't have the words to do it.

3. A character loves dad jokes, but their friends don't, so they don't say them out loud.

It Doesn't Get Any Realer Than This
All About Creative Nonfiction
By Gina Loveless

The fun thing about creative nonfiction is that you get to tell a story based on facts that already exist. The tricky thing about creative nonfiction is that you get to tell a story based on facts that already exist.

But that's okay. Let's break down creative nonfiction so that it feels easy and fun.

The first step to creative nonfiction is picking a topic. Maybe you want to write about someone from history that means a lot to you. Or maybe you want to write about a period in history that's really interesting to you. Or about a scientific piece of information that surprises you.

No matter what, you want to start with something specific.

Next is research.

The internet can be a helpful place to find research. But it's important to do two things: 1) only go online and do research with the help of a trusted adult and 2) look for certain key details. You want to make sure the website you're reading is reputable. In this case, that means finding out if it's a good non-biased source.

How can you tell if something is reputable? Check to see if the main address ends in .edu or .org. If not, are they an authority on this subject? Do they write a lot about this topic?

Once you've gathered at least 10—yes 10!—different websites, you'll want to read through these websites and pull pieces of information that are interesting. Make sure you keep track of which information came from which websites.

Now that you have all your interesting information, and you have the sites to back them up, it's time to write what you've learned about in your own words. Think about what you've learned and how you can help others learn about your topic in an interesting way.

Nonfiction Writing Activities

It's time to take on the real world!

Start a Research Journal
By Celesta

You'll need to gather many facts as you work on creative nonfiction! Writers often refer back to their research as they write, so you'll want to keep track of your research and where you found your facts.

Start a research journal for your current writing project. It can be as simple as a spiral bound notebook or as fancy as a bound journal or a book you make yourself. Your research journal can also be a saved document on your computer. Just be sure to label it and save it in a place where you can always find it. As you research and make notes about the important things you learn, remember to write down everything you'll need to find that resource again and to include it in your **bibliography.**

A **bibliography** is a list of all the sources the author used to write a piece of nonfiction. It lists, in detail, where the author got their facts. These are the things you will need for each source you use in your research:

1. The author of the book, article, or blog post

2. The title of the book, article, or blog post

3. The pages of the book, article, or blog post that you are referencing

4. The publisher

5. The city where the publisher is located

6. The date the book, article, or blog post was published

7. The website url (if the source was online)

Ask a Librarian
By Celesta

What is a nonfiction topic you want to write about? Is it a person, place, or an event? Perhaps it's something unusual about nature. Now, go to your school library or local public library and ask a librarian for help researching books about your topic.

Librarians can show you how to find reliable information that is useful for what you're writing. Next, look through the books you find and make notes of things you learn. Be sure to jot down the title and author of each book you use so you know where you got your information. (Check out my note about bibliographies on the previous page.)

To get you started, I've listed some examples below of actual topics I researched as I wrote my novels *The Elephant's Girl* and *Tips for Magicians*. Even though I was writing fictional stories, I needed information about nonfiction topics so I could include realistic details.

Nonfiction topic examples:

- Elephant herds in the wild
- Elephants in zoos and their diets
- Elephant emotions and communication
- Caitlin O'Connell, conservation biologist and elephant expert
- How a steam engine works
- Categories of tornadoes

- Birds of prey
- Falconry in the desert
- Apprentice falconers
- Wildlife in the Mojave Desert
- Unusual painting styles and how they are done
- Tips that master magicians share with aspiring magicians
- How to do card tricks

Hidden Figures
By Sarah

Who is someone from history you think more people should know about? If you're not sure how to find someone, that's ok! Just start by asking yourself some questions. Who invented the microwave? Who discovered bacteria or blue whales? Who was the first woman in space? The first Black person to win the Kentucky Derby or graduate from Harvard? Were there any female pirates? Who performed the first open-heart surgery?

Find a question that is interesting to *you*! Your parents/guardians, teachers, and librarians can help you find the answers. Then write down everything you learn about this interesting person!

Write a Nonfiction Poem!
By Sarah

Nonfiction writing can be just as fun and beautiful as a story or a poem! Pick something you're interested in—maybe it's rocket ships or the ancient Mongols or dumbo octopuses (look them up, they're so cute!) Make a list of all the cool things you learn about your chosen topic. Then take that list and rewrite it as a poem, paying attention to line breaks and word choice. Now you can talk about robots or photosynthesis or Sacajawea and sound both smart *and* lyrical!

Reinvent the Mouse Trap
By Gina

Plenty of good ideas already exist, but they need YOUR unique spin on them to become something special. With *Puberty Is Gross But Also Really Awesome*, there were already lots of puberty books out there, but none of them used humorous language and were all-gender inclusive. How can you put your take on something that already exists?

Cookbooks
By Gina

Tell the story of your family history through a cookbook. Ask your family members for their favorite recipes. Interview them about where the recipe came from and its history in your family. Write every second of it down. Then come up with your own recipes, inspired by their stories, and write down where your ideas for them came from.

Memoirs of a Genius
By PJ

"I'm not going to tell the story the way it happened. I'm going to tell it the way I remember it."

-Great Expectations [1998 Film]

Memoirs and autobiographies do similar things–they tell the story of the writer's life—but they do it in different ways. Autobiographies tend to tell the stories in chronological order and with an emphasis on facts. Memoirs are looser in structure and, like the name implies, are more grounded in memories. And, as we all know, memories are rooted in emotions. So, for this exercise I want you to write a memoir of last school year. The key is to focus on the moments that made big impressions on you and how you felt–and maybe still feel–about them.

- Did you make or lose a friend?

- Did you pass a test you thought you'd fail or fail a test you were sure you'd pass?

- Did an author visit your school?

Write about anything and everything that has stayed with you.

How to Do the Thing
By PJ

Do you know how to do something that others don't, like paint a beautiful watercolor landscape or build the perfect Minecraft world? Writing a How To allows you to share your expertise with others. Here's how you do it:

1. Quickly write up your process on a sheet of paper.

2. Go through and make sure you've got each step in the right order.

3. Do any research you need to do.

4. Rewrite it by hand or on the computer.

Give it a shot.

.... **Sarah says:**

Remember that your special skill might be unexpected! Maybe you're really great at microwaving the perfect popcorn. Maybe you're great at telling jokes or befriending cats. These are also special skills! Remember these hidden talents as you think about what skill to share.

Poetry: Rhyme, Time, Chime, and Other Stuff That Doesn't Rhyme, Too

By Sarah Allen

So...poetry. There are a *lot* of misconceptions about it. People might think poetry is a *big deal* and *very serious*. People might think poetry is just stuff that rhymes. People might think they're not smart enough to write poetry. None of those things are true!

You might think that to write poetry you need to know all sorts of *types* of poetry like sonnets and haikus and villanelles. You might think you need to know fancy terms like *iambic pentameter* and *onomatopoeia*. (That's a fun word to say, isn't it?) Those are all good things to know about, if you want to. But if you just want to get started writing poetry, there are really only two things to pay attention to. And they're not as tricky as you might think.

Those two things are **line** and **sound**.

Line

Normal writing uses regular sentences. You don't think about where the sentences stop on the page, because regular sentences go from one side of the page to the other, like this. The computer even does it for you. Easy.

Poetry uses lines instead. Poetry doesn't
go across the page. It stops
and moves down
and down
whenever it chooses.

Think about where you want to stop
your lines. In the middle
of a sentence? At the end?
Maybe in the
middle of a wo-
rd?

Why did you choose to stop there? What do the words in that one line make you think and feel?

Let's look at an example. Take a look at this poem by William Carlos Williams:

The Red Wheelbarrow
so much depends
upon

a red wheel

barrow

glazed with rain
water

beside the white
chickens.

Why do you think Williams chose to end the lines when he did? What did you feel after the first line? After the first stanza? Did it make you think...*so much depends on WHAT?* Did you like the trick in the second stanza where you think the line ends on *wheel* but he then he adds *barrow* in the next line? There are no right or wrong answers about where to end your lines. But it's always good to carefully think about how your lines impact the way the reader reads your poem.

<u>Sound</u>

Say this out-loud: Peter Piper picked a peck of pickled peppers.

What do the sounds make you think of? All the 'p' sounds might make you think of popping gum. Maybe that's the sound you wanted in your poem, but maybe it isn't.

Now say these words out loud: cellar door.

Don't think about what it means. Just close your eyes and say the words three times out loud, listening to the sounds as if it was music. It's kind of a pretty word, isn't it? The sounds make me think of fields of unicorns.

When you choose the words in your poem, think about the sounds they make, not just what the words mean. Then when you read it out loud, it will sound as beautiful as a song!

Let's look at another example. Take a look at a bit of this poem by Gerard Manley Hopkins. As you read this, don't try to understand the words. Gerard Manley Hopkins uses very strange, big words that even I don't really understand. But that's ok! Don't try to understand, just read it out loud and pay attention to the way it sounds, the same as when you said the Peter Piper rhyme. Just listen and see what the sounds make you feel. Pay attention to how he repeats words and vowels and consonants.

The Windhover

I caught this morning morning's minion, king-
    dom of daylight's dauphin, dapple-dawn-drawn Falcon,
in his riding
    Of the rolling level underneath him steady air, and
striding
    High there, how he rung upon the rein of a wimpling
wing
    In his ecstasy! then off, off forth on swing,
    As a skate's heel sweeps smooth on a bow-bend: the
hurl and gliding
    Rebuffed the big wind. My heart in hiding
    Stirred for a bird, – the achieve of, the mastery of the
thing!

What did you think? Sounds pretty interesting, huh? I think so! Without any melody, this poem, to me, sounds like music. As you pay attention to the sounds your words make, your poems can sound like music too!

Remember: there is no right or wrong way to write poetry. Did you notice how different those two poems are? Poetry can be serious or silly, long or short, rhymed or not rhymed. It can be loud and thundery like crashing cymbals, or soft and bubbly as a stream of water. It can be about the crow outside your window, a witch's nose, a circus, a dragon, a computer game, a robot, whatever you want! When you have fun writing your poetry, people will have fun reading it.

Poetry Activities

Not just rhyme

Pleiades Poem
By PJ

A pleiades poem is simple and fun to write. It's seven lines that all start with the same sound/letter as the one-word title.

For help with words that begin with the same letter check out the website, WordFinder by YourDictionary.

Example:

"Dogs" by PJ Gardner

Dopey and weird.
Dirty and stinky.
Digging in the yard.
Determined to lick my face.
Dragging me when we go for a walk.
Delightfully snuggling when I sleep.
Devoted to making me feel loved.

Haiku
By PJ

Haiku originated in Japan in the thirteenth century, but evolved over time into the classic form we know today. They are just three lines. The first line is five syllables. The second line is seven syllables. And the last line is five syllables again.

Example:

"Rain Makes Me Smile" by PJ Gardner

Gray skies bring the rain.
Water to nourish the seeds.
So flowers will grow.

Ekphrasis
By Gina

Write a poem based on a picture or of a work of art. Go to a museum or look at a painting or picture that's hung in your home and write down everything and anything that comes to mind.

Example:

D.G. Stouter, *On Point,* 1854

"Snack" by Gina Loveless

I see you,
little fluttery things,
pecking and squabbling about.

Don't you know
that you are food!
That I am hungry!

Fear me, snack!
For I am twice your height
and twice as likely to snap
you in half as an afternoon treat.

Concrete Poem
By Gina

Write a poem about a cloud. Then reconfigure the poem so it looks like a cloud. Write a poem about a tree and then make it look like a tree. When you write a poem that looks like a shape or pattern, that's a concrete poem.

Example:

"Small Tree" by Gina Loveless

A
green
staple at
the holidays
makes parents and
children rejoice. But not
cats.

Poetry Can Tell Stories!
By Sarah

Did you know that sometimes whole books are written with poems? Maybe you've read some of those books. Aren't they great?

Try it out yourself. Think of the most important moment in your character's day. It could be anything! Maybe it's when they get in a fight with their friend at school. Maybe it's when they find the dragon's hoard. Write that scene in normal writing, like you usually would.

Now try writing it as a poem. It's the same story, the same moment, just told in a different way. Pay attention to the lines and where you end them. Pay attention to the sounds the words make. Maybe you want to choose a different word because of the way it sounds.

Now you have two versions of the scene. What do you like about the regular version? What do you like about the poem version?

Extra Ordinary
By Sarah

One of the best things about poetry is that it can turn seemingly unimportant, everyday things into something special, wondrous, and even magical. Try looking around you and finding something ordinary. Something you see every day and don't even notice. Now put it in a poem! Write about it as beautifully as you can and try seeing it in new and unusual ways. What does it remind you of? What does this object do for you that makes a big difference in your life? You may not ever look at that object the same way again!

Poetic Feelings
By Celesta

Poetry can be a great way to express what you feel. Try writing a poem about a feeling you have had. What does the feeling remind you of? What senses are associated with this feeling? Taste, smell, color, sound, temperature? Find something in the world that you can use to represent that feeling and include it in your poem. In the example below, I used cotton candy to represent joy and happy memories.

"The Visit" by Celesta Rimington

The world is pink
when Grandma arrives

We tell secrets
and jokes

and our sweet
cotton candy laughter

sticks
to us
til long after

Some tools that writers use to spice up their writing are called simile and metaphor. You've probably already heard about these literary devices, but here is a reminder:

A simile is when you compare two things using the words "like" or "as." For example:

My grandma's red bean chili is like fire on my tongue.

The dog escaped through the gate as quick as a burglar on the run.

A metaphor is when you compare two things by saying one thing "is" the other, when that isn't literally correct. One thing is a symbol for the other. For example:

The breeze through the trees is a lullaby that sings me to sleep.

My older brother is a couch potato.

Diamante: A Shape Poem About Opposites
By Celesta

This poem makes a fun diamond shape on your page, it doesn't have to rhyme, and it's easy if you follow the directions!

First, choose two opposites to write about. Some examples to try are light and dark, summer and winter, or cat and dog. Next, choose which of the opposites will start the poem and which will end it. You might start with the word dark and end with the word light.

Your diamante poem will be seven lines long with the first and seventh lines composed of only one word—your opposite words. Write the seven lines of your poem like this:

Line 1: first opposite word (or topic)

Line 2: two adjectives to describe line 1

Line 3: three verbs that end in *-ing* to describe line 1

Line 4: four nouns or noun phrases that connect your two opposites

Line 5: three verbs that end in *-ing* to describe line 7

Line 6: two adjectives to describe line 7

Line 7: second opposite word (or topic)

Here is mine:

"Silent Surprise" by Celesta Rimington

mouse
small, furry
scurrying, scampering, squeaking
wild, free, quick, hungry
slithering, hiding, waiting
long, patient
snake

I hope you'll try this yourself and have fun!

Editing: If It Ain't Broke, Don't...
Oh Wait, It Is Broken
By Sarah Allen

Now we get to talk about the most funnest part of writing—EDITING!

What?! You don't *like* editing? You think it's hard and confusing and boring? Ok, ok, I understand what you're saying. I don't really care about spelling myself, and probably couldn't tell you much about what certain grammar rules are called. So let's all do a big Grammar Groan and get that out of the way. Uuuuggghhhhh.

Ok, feel better? Because I'm here to tell you that editing really, truly can be fun! It's sort of like when you draw a picture, and you finally fill in all the colors and get the last touches of shading just right. That's what editing is for your story. There will be lots of people to help you with grammar and spelling later on, and editing is much, *much* more than just knowing your bears from your bares.

When you're done with your story, the next part of a writer's job is to make it the best story they can. To do that, it's a good idea to take a nice long look at what you've written and ask yourself some important questions. If you start with the big questions, then the medium, then the small, by the time you're done, your story will shine like a beautiful painting!

- *Big Questions:* Does the plot of my story make sense, or did I forget some parts? What does my character discover about themselves by the end of the story? (Is it that they're braver, kinder, or cleverer than they thought they were?) Are there parts where my setting is confusing?

- *Medium Questions:* Does every scene in my story matter, or are there some I could take out and it wouldn't change the story? Does my character really go for what they want in every scene, or do they just kind of sit there? Does my main character sound different from the other characters?

- *Small Questions:* Did I choose the most descriptive verb for this sentence? (Did your character hop or did they bounce?) Did I use lots of my senses in this story, and not just sight? (What do things smell like and sound like?) Did I use the same word too many times? (I just always use 'just' so many times I just can't help it!) Do I have some short sentences and some long sentences, to keep things interesting? And finally, (cue another Grammar Groan) is my grammar correct, and are my words spelled right?

Now that you've made your story the best you can, it's time to get help from some other people. That brings me to the last thing you need to know about editing: When a teacher, parent, guardian, or friend tells you some things you might fix in your story, that doesn't mean it's a bad story! And it doesn't mean that you're a bad writer.

Think of your favorite book of all time. Got it? Well, that book had lots and lots of big, medium, and small things to fix before it could become your favorite book. I *promise*. And with these editing questions and with help from smart teachers, trusted adults, and friends, your story is going to be amazing too!

A Peek at Professional Edits!

To show you what some of the edits look like when you're working with a professional editor and a professional publisher, here is an example from my horror novel, *The Nightmare House*. The first example is what it looked like with notes from the editor. The second example is what it looked like after those edits, in the final version. As you can see, it takes a lot of smart people to make a book shine!

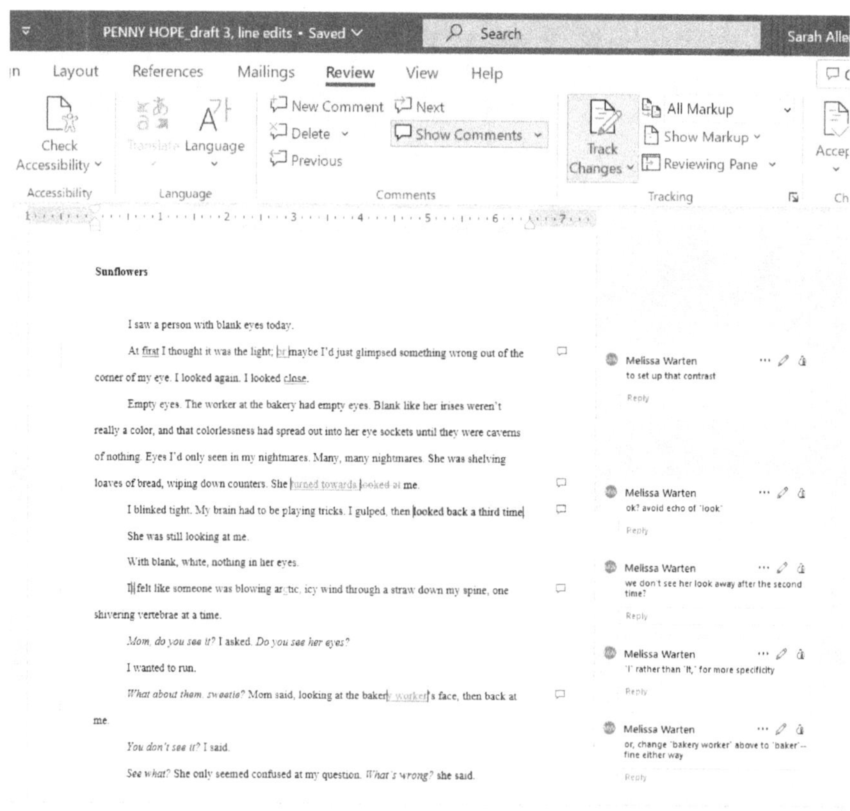

Sunflowers

I saw a person with blank eyes today.

At first I thought it was the light, or maybe I'd just glimpsed something wrong out of the corner of my eye. I looked again. I looked closer.

Empty eyes. The baker had empty eyes. Blank like her irises weren't really a color, and that colorlessness had spread out into her eye sockets until they were caverns of nothing. Eyes I'd seen only in my nightmares. Many, many nightmares.

She was shelving loaves of bread, wiping down counters. She turned toward me and I couldn't help but look away.

I blinked tight. My brain had to be playing tricks. I gulped, then looked back a third time.

She was still looking at me.

With blank, white, nothing in her eyes.

I felt like someone was blowing arctic, icy wind through a straw down my spine, one shivering vertebra at a time.

Mom, do you see it? I asked. *Do you see her eyes?*

I wanted to run.

What about them, sweetie? Mom said, looking at the baker's face, then back at me.

You don't see it? I said.

See what? She seemed confused at my question. *What's wrong?* she said.

Editing Activities

Not as terrible as you think

The Pyramid of Abstraction
by Sarah

Let's talk about two words: concrete and abstract. A concrete word or idea is something that's very solid, descriptive, and specific. An abstract word or idea is more vague, obscure, and not very exact. For example, if I tell you to think of sadness, you might have some ideas, but not something you can visualize or hold in your hand. And I'm probably thinking of sadness in a totally different way than you! But what if I tell you to think of finding a rip in your favorite shirt. Now we're getting closer to thinking of the same thing! Or what if I tell you to think of burying a pet hedgehog in the backyard. Those are both sad things, but very different kinds of sadness!

Your story will be most powerful and effective when you use concrete words and sentences instead of abstract. One great way to edit your story is to go through and ask yourself if there are words and sentences that you could move down the Pyramid of Abstraction–away from abstract, and more towards the concrete. (Find the image on the next page.) See how the pyramid is mostly built of the concrete stuff? That's how your story should be too!

PYRAMID OF ABSTRACTION

Find A Reader!
By Sarah

Now that you've written your story, and followed all the activities in this section to make it the best you can, the next step is to find a reader! This is the best thing you can do for your story, because there are things we simply don't notice about our own stories–like plot holes or spelling mistakes–until someone else points it out. That's normal!

Find a trusted parent, guardian, teacher, or friend to read your story. I know this can be scary! I always worry about sharing my work too, but it's important to be brave and let other people help us. That's how we improve!

Ask your trusted reader to tell you two things:

- What did they really like about your story? What worked well?
- What did they find confusing about your story? What did they wonder about?

They don't need to tell you exactly how to fix those question spots. But after they've given you some questions to think about, now *you* can figure how to fix those questions and make your story even better!

Kill Your Darlings
By Gina

"Kill your darlings" is a famous line in editing. It means to cut or get rid of your favorite lines. Or a favorite section. Or a favorite paragraph. As writers, sometimes we get very attached to certain lines, sections, paragraphs, etc., even though they aren't helping the book or story or poem move forward like it should.

Create a new document. Go through and cut out your favorite lines from your story or book or poem and place them in that new document. Re-read the book or story or poem and see if it makes sense without those lines. If you absolutely above all else MUST keep them in, then go back and put them back in. But if your story is still strong without it, then you're better off keeping that darling out of the work.

Consistency is Key
By Gina

After you've written your first draft, when you're reading back through your story to edit, pay attention to one character at a time. Are they being consistent with their language? With their actions? With the way they move about in your world? If they're yelling at their best friend, and they're typically a shy character, this is a scene you may need to edit. Check to see if each of your characters are being who they usually are.

Thesaurus for the Win
By PJ

Every writer has a word (or ten) that they tend to overuse. When that happens it's time to turn to your handy dandy thesaurus, which lists alternate words that mean the same thing. These are called synonyms. You can find a free thesaurus online but, as always, check with your grown up before going on the internet.

Look up the following words and write down some synonyms:

- Sad

- Angry

- Hurt

- Loud

- Lonely

The Power of the Notecard
By PJ

Keeping track of all the changes you need to make in your manuscript can get overwhelming, that's why I use notecards to organize my edits. Sometimes my notes are very specific like: "Make sure the dog's name is the same throughout." And sometimes they're more general like: "Make Toby more likable."

For this exercise, take a large, lined notecard and write down everything you need to change or fix. Start with the easiest things first. When you finish the edit, cross it off the list.

First Pages Detective
By Celesta

Think of your favorite stories. Find or borrow a copy of one of your favorite books and take a close look at the first two pages. Got it? Now, read the first two sentences of that book out loud to yourself. Did those first two sentences make you want to keep reading? Why?

Now, I don't know which book you are holding. But if it is one of your favorite stories, I have a pretty good idea of why you like it so much and why you read beyond the first two pages.

Strong story beginnings do three things very well. First, they **reveal something about the character** that makes the reader interested and want to know more. Second, they **present a conflict** that makes readers curious. And third, they **plant questions** in the readers' minds. As humans, we are naturally curious, and we want to find answers to our questions. So, when the beginning of a story sparks our curiosity, we are easily hooked and want to keep reading!

Now, look at the first few lines of your own story. Do you have these three important elements of a strong beginning? If you do, can you revise them to make them stronger? If you don't, look at these examples below for ideas. Even in your first few lines, you can:

- **Show your readers something about your main character**

- **Present a conflict (even if it isn't the main conflict yet)**

- **Start a question or two in your readers' minds.**

Here are some examples to help you:

You can do this with dialogue like this beginning line from the classic book *Charlotte's Web* by E.B. White:

"Where's Papa going with that ax?" said Fern to her mother as they were setting the table for breakfast.

In this one line, we know that Fern is probably the main character. We know Fern is helpful (she is setting the table) and she cares about what is going on around her (she notices something unusual and asks a question.) We also get our hint of conflict (Papa is carrying an ax), and we as the readers already have our own questions like Fern. We read on because we, too, want to know what is going on with the ax.

You can do this without dialogue, too. You can use your character's voice and point of view like this example from my book *The Elephant's Girl:*

The wind and I have a complicated relationship. Because of the wind, I'm the girl without a birthday, without a name, without a beginning to my story.

From these two sentences, we know the main character is a girl who has questions about who she is. We also get our hint of conflict with the wind. This leads the reader to ask questions like "What happened with the wind?" and "Will she find out who she is, and how?"

Now, **be a first-pages detective.** Try out different ways to revise the beginning lines of your story to show character, introduce conflict, and plant questions for your readers. Keep those three things in mind for the first few pages of your story as well.

Verbs Beat Adverbs in a Wrestling Match
By Celesta

Here is an activity to do once you have made your larger edits and you're ready to shine up the words you use. This is one of my favorite ways to polish sentences!

Words that tell how, when, or where something happens are called adverbs. They're intended to strengthen or support the verbs, adjectives, and other adverbs we use. Some examples of adverbs are: sometimes, obviously, happily, silently, and almost.

We need adverbs, but not all the time.

For example, Julius can write something, or he can write it quickly. The word *write* is the verb and the word *quickly* is the adverb. The adverb tells us *how* Julius wrote something. Not all adverbs end in *-ly*, but many of them do, and that can make them easy to spot.

Come closer, though, because I have a secret for you. If you find the ideal verb or adjective in the first place, you don't need those adverbs getting in the way. What is a stronger verb that will triumph over that adverb in a wrestling match?

Instead of: Julius *wrote the list quickly* in his notebook.
Try this: Julius *scribbled* the list in his notebook.

Instead of: She thought Andrea was *really funny*.
Try this: She thought Andrea was *hilarious*.

Look for adverbs in your writing and try using a thesaurus as PJ suggested to help you find stronger verbs and adjectives to take their place. The vibrant words that mean exactly what you want to say will always win!

Make That Book!
Tools to Share Your Stories
By Celesta Rimington and Gina Loveless

Now that you've followed Sarah's fantastic advice and used your editing tools from the activity pages, what comes next? Are you excited to see your story in print and hoping to have a finished book to hold in your hands? Do you want to see your story in a library? Maybe you want a great way to share your story with friends and family. We (Celesta and Gina) have several tools for you to get your story in the hands of readers. We'll start the list with the easiest ones and end with the most advanced methods. With help and support from your parents, guardians, teachers, and librarians, you have so many options at your fingertips!

Handmade Books:

There are so many options when it comes to the world of handmade books. You can literally take a single sheet of paper and turn it into a little mini book. You can fold multiple pieces of paper over and staple them and make a simple, makeshift booklet. Or you can use special glues and wax-covered yarns and make beautiful creations for you and your readers. The choices are endless!

Here are some places to get started with handmade books:
- *How to Make Books: Fold, Cut & Stitch Your Way to a One-of-a-Kind Book* by Esther K. Smith
- *Re-Bound: Creating Handmade Books from Recycled and Repurposed Materials* by Jeannine Stein
- *Making Handmade Books: 100+ Bindings, Structures & Forms* by Alisa Golden
- "How to Make a Book From a Single Sheet of Paper" https://www.youtube.com/watch?v=bHa6kR2SZok

<u>Print and Bind at Copy Shops:</u>

Copy shops like Staples or FedEx Office and Print Centers will bind books for you at a cost. You choose from styles like coil binding or saddle stitch. Ask to look at examples of the bindings so you know what yours will look like.

<u>Talk to Your Librarians:</u>

Did you know that some libraries will make a section of student-created books? If you ask your librarians, they may have a place to shelve your book and will enter your book in the library system so that other readers can check it out! If your library has a program like this, you will want to ask the librarians for ideas about how to bind your book in a way that will help it last as long as possible.

<u>Enter Creative Writing Contests and Submit to Magazines:</u>

Some creative writing contests for young writers publish the winners in magazines in print or online. Here is a website that lists magazines that publish writing by children and teens.

<u>https://authorspublish.com/22-magazines-that-publish-writing-by-children-and-teens/</u>

Print Your Book Professionally:

This option costs more money than the others, and you will need an adult to create the account and help ensure your book looks the way you want. Perhaps you can coordinate a fundraiser with your library or school to raise money for you and other creative writers to print your stories. A few websites adults can help you with to print small orders of paperbacks and hardcovers are:

https://www.lulu.com/

https://www.bookbaby.com/

Self-Publish With Support From a Trusted Adult:

Writers can self-publish using the websites we mentioned above or with companies like Ingram Spark or Amazon Kindle Direct Publishing that print and distribute books anywhere books are sold. However, you must be 18 years of age or older to create accounts with these companies and use their services. Be sure to talk to an adult you trust about these options if you'd like to learn more.

<h1 style="text-align:center">Query Literary Agents:</h1>

When we (Celesta and Gina) were in elementary and middle school, we desperately wanted published authors to tell us exactly *how* to get published. Now, as we do author visits with students today, we always get questions about this! If you want to publish a book through traditional publishers, you'll need a professional literary agent to represent you as an author. This is a longer process than the options listed above, and you need a parent or guardian to assist you if you are under 18 years old. It takes most authors several years to find an agent and sell their book to a publisher (with plenty of rejections), but when you have the involvement and support of adults you trust, and you feel you are ready, here are some ways to go about it.

.... **Celesta says:**

Beware of any agent or agency that offers to represent you for a fee! A reputable agent will not charge money to represent you. They only get paid when they sell your book to a publisher, and even then, it is typically 15% of the money you receive for your book.

Check out the acknowledgements in the backs of books you like and see if the author thanked their agent. Then, review the agency websites and make a list of agents who are looking for the kinds of stories you write. Agency websites give specific instructions about how to query an agent for representation, so writers need to carefully follow those directions. Ask a parent or guardian to review the process with you. Query Tracker is a helpful online resource for finding and learning about literary agents. Many articles online share tips about writing effective and professional query letters. As always, ask your adults' permission before going online.

https://querytracker.net/

Remember, it takes most authors a lot of time to find an agent, and it is common to receive many rejections. If you want to avoid the rejections for now and have more creative control over your work, try the options closer to the top of this list.

A Final Note:

The process of sharing your stories should be fun, and it doesn't have to cost you anything! There is no one right way to share or publish your creative writing. These are just some of the tools to help!

Rejection is for Winners!
Tools for Winning at the Ups and Downs of Writing
By Sarah, PJ, Gina, and Celesta

Sharing your creative work can be exciting, but it can also be disappointing at times. Here are some stories from our writing lives and ways we deal with the ups and downs.

PJ

Writing is wonderful, but publishing often is not. There's a lot of negativity, from query rejections to harsh reviews. And sometimes it can make you feel like giving up. I have a secret weapon I use to fight the publishing blues—an encouragement playlist. It's a bunch of songs that make me feel strong and hopeful. I listen to them and immediately feel better. And then sometimes I'll hear that song on the radio, and it will inspire me to keep going. Whether you make an encouragement playlist for yourself or leave happy thoughts on sticky notes around your house, make sure to find ways of lifting yourself up when things get hard.

Gina

Rejection can come at many different times throughout this writing journey. For me, it didn't come at the beginning. I queried my top pick agents, and I got lucky enough to have one of them pick me back. I did get passes from a number of agents during this time, too, but I was able to hold onto hope that one of the other agents on my list might get back to me. (Which he did! Thanks Alec Shane!)

Rejection came for me at a time I didn't expect. I had sold five books, and I thought I had a sixth on its way. But the sixth didn't come. For more than four years. I auditioned* and queried with over 15 projects during these four years, and didn't sell a book. But I kept going and I keep going, even though it's been hard, because I still have more stories to tell, and I believe that I'll be able to tell more stories to kids like you.

When you audition for a book, it's kind of like when an actress or actor auditions for a movie or TV show. They have to rehearse a section of the screenplay, and then present it in front of people involved in the movie or TV show, to see if they want to use them for the movie or TV show. When you audition for a book, you usually write an outline of what your version of the book would look like, and then a sample chapter, to showcase what your voice sounds like. The people involved in having the book made review many different auditions, and then decide which one they want to use for the book.

Celesta

I'm going to share with you the hardest rejection I had before I became a published author and how I handled it. I hope it helps you when you are disappointed that something didn't go the way you hoped.

Before I found my agent, I wrote two completed novels and two that were partially completed. I met an agent at a writing conference who was interested enough in my second completed novel that he wanted to read the whole thing! He took a really long time to get back to me, and when he finally did, it was an impersonal rejection (or a form letter.) I was very sad and discouraged because I'd thought this agent was so excited about my book when we met.

Soon after that, I received a rejection from a small publisher for the same book. This was after an editor at that small publisher had told me how much they loved my book. At first, I thought maybe I wasn't good enough to do what I wanted to do as a writer.

Never think that!

When you're discouraged, be kind to yourself and tell someone you trust. They'll help lift you up and remind you that your rejection has nothing to do with your amazing ideas and your value.

I told my good friend I was disappointed, and she met me at the park with some homemade brownies! Friends and trusted adults are the best!

Later, I went out to a restaurant to get my favorite dinner. I took time to notice the smells and sounds around me and wrote them down. I wrote in my writing journal all the reasons I love to write fiction. I jotted down new ideas for new books. I brainstormed. And then, I took a break from writing for a few days and read books I love and watched a few movies. I gave my brain new stories to focus on—ones that make me happy and make me want to keep writing.

Most importantly, even though I took a little break, I didn't give up. Guess what story I wrote next? My debut novel *The Elephant's Girl*. Out of my rejection and disappointment came a great middle grade book that I'm so happy I wrote!

A **form letter** is a piece of mail or an email that is not personally addressed to you and is a standard, identical response sent to a lot of people. An example of a form letter rejection I received from an agent began this way:

Dear Author,
Thank you for your interest in our agency. Unfortunately, your story is not a good fit for our list...

See how the letter did not include my name and sounds like something they send to a lot of people? That's a form letter. It can be discouraging, but please, keep learning and keep trying!

Sarah

I've known I wanted to be a writer ever since I was little. Maybe you have too. (If not, that's ok!) I did a lot of research about being a writer and knew that getting published took a *long* time and meant a *lot* of rejection. I'm glad I knew that, because...well, it was certainly true for me.

I wrote my first book in college. I sent it out to agents and got dozens of rejections. I wrote another book and sent it to agents. Dozens more rejections. Third book—still more rejections. I spent about six or seven years sending out those books and collecting hundreds of rejection emails. I could probably wallpaper my room with them!

Finally, I wrote my fourth book, *What Stars Are Made Of*. That book also got many rejections from agents, but then it also got a YES! Four yesses, in fact! Suddenly, after all those years and all those rejections, I had four agents who wanted to help me publish my book. I chose the one I thought was the best fit, and then guess what...*more* rejections. This time from publishers. But this time it didn't take seven years, only a few months. Then we found a publisher and finally I got my book on the shelves!

Here's the tough news—I still get rejections. A lot of them. I get rejections when I send out stories and poems to magazines. My agent and I are sending a new book to publishers right now, and it's getting lots of rejections.

So how do you keep going? How do you keep going when so many people are telling you no?

Well, there are two things I always remember.

1. **It's not about me:** When someone rejects my book, it absolutely *doesn't* mean it's a bad book, or that I'm a bad writer. In fact, I've had people who *loved* my writing and thought my book was fantastic, and they *still* had to reject it for a million other reasons. So even though it's hard not to take rejection personally, remember that it doesn't mean you're a bad writer.

2. **Thank you, next:** When I get a no, I try to immediately turn around and think about what's next. That can mean a lot of things. Maybe the *next* agent will love your book and say yes. Maybe the *next* book idea you're excited about will be The One. Maybe after you get some different books published, you can come back to this one and get it published *next*. (This happened to me!) The key thing is to keep moving forward to the next person, the next exciting idea, and the next project.

Strange and Unusual Writing Prompts
By Sarah and PJ

Okay, now that you have all those tools, it's time to play. Remember, there's no one right way to write a story. In fact, there are dozens. Now that you've learned about character, plots, and all those other fun tools, try using them in some unusual and funky ways!

- Epistolary (Letters): Have your main character write a letter to a family member about something that happened at school.

- Diary Entries: Your main character has a secret, and a diary is the only place they can share it.

- Recipe: Your character decides to cook/bake something they used to make with their grandmother. What's written on the recipe card?

- Texts: Your character is somewhere they're not supposed to be. Then they get a text from Mom. What does that text conversation look like?

- To Do Lists: Tell us about your character's day through their to-do list. What's on their list that isn't on anybody else's?

- How To's: Write a how-to manual teaching a robot how to tell a joke. Write a how-to manual guiding an alien through a human activity they don't understand.

- Discord Chats: Your character is in a discord chat for a class at school, and someone is there who shouldn't be.

- Newspaper Articles: Your character is cleaning out the attic and discovers an article about their dad that reveals hidden secrets.

- Your character is convinced that the lunch lady is stealing pepperonis from the pizza. She decides to write a hard-hitting investigative report for the school newspaper. Write the article!

- Graphic Novels/Comics: Have your main character create a comic book about their superhero alter ego. Stick figures are ok!

- Wikipedia Entries: Have your character create a Wikipedia page for their favorite video game character.

- Stories in Verse: Write the first paragraph of your story. Now try writing it in verse!

- Change Perspective (By Gina): Is your story told in first person perspective? Is everything I this and I that? Try changing the perspective of the story, by making it third person. If your story is already in third person, try changing it to first. What changes when you write it like this? What can you learn about the characters in that way?

- A Song (By Gina): Instead of telling your story through paragraphs, tell your story through song. Write the words like a lyric. Maybe rhyme some endings. If you're musically talented, add some drumbeats or guitar licks to it.

Connect With Us!

We hope you have enjoyed *Tools, Not Rules: A Writing Guide for Young Creatives*. We want to hear about your writing and how you've used this book! You can find our other books at the links below and learn more about us through our websites.

We also provide school and classroom author visits! Ask your parents, teachers, or librarians to contact us at

toolsnotrules@gmail.com

or through our websites.

Celesta:

Author Website:
celestarimington.com

Books:

https://www.rhcbooks.com/authors/2198105/celesta-rimington

Gina:

Author Website:

lovelesswriting.com

Books:

https://www.rhcbooks.com/authors/2184108/gina-loveless

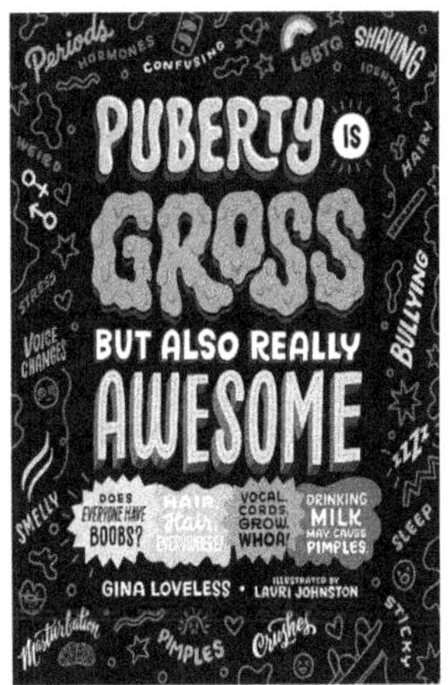

PJ:

Author Website:

pjgardnerswitzer.com

Books:

https://www.harpercollins.com/blogs/authors/pj-gardner

Sarah:

Author Website:
sarahallenbooks.com

Newsletter:
sarahallen.substack.com

Books:

https://us.macmillan.com/author/sarahallen

The End